USAWC STRATEGY RESEARCH PROJECT

TORTURE AND THE WAR ON TERRORISM:
TIME TO THINK THE UNTHINKABLE?

by

Lieutenant Colonel Douglas A. Galipeau
United States Air Force

Dr. David Perry
Project Advisor

This SRP is submitted in partial fulfillment of the requirements of the Master of Strategic Studies Degree. The U.S. Army War College is accredited by the Commission on Higher Education of the Middle States Association of Colleges and Schools, 3624 Market Street, Philadelphia, PA 19104, (215) 662-5606. The Commission on Higher Education is an institutional accrediting agency recognized by the U.S. Secretary of Education and the Council for Higher Education Accreditation.

The views expressed in this student academic research paper are those of the author and do not reflect the official policy or position of the Department of the Army, Department of Defense, or the U.S. Government.

U.S. Army War College
CARLISLE BARRACKS, PENNSYLVANIA 17013

ii

ABSTRACT

AUTHOR: Lieutenant Colonel Douglas A. Galipeau

TITLE: Torture And The War On Terrorism: Time To Think The Unthinkable?

FORMAT: Strategy Research Project

DATE: 18 March 2005   PAGES: 28   CLASSIFICATION: Unclassified

Recent incidents at Abu Ghraib prison brought to light one of the more vexing and potentially troublesome issues the U.S. is likely to face in this conflict: Does the nature of the War on Terror justify the use of extraordinary measures, i.e., torture, in our effort to defeat the enemy? This paper begins with a brief review of the events leading up to the scandal at Abu Ghraib to include the potential influence of policy discussions at the highest levels of government. Following that background discussion, I identify some of the pitfalls associated with defining torture and review some of the major schools of thought on the subject. I then examine the completely antithetical nature of the use of torture in relation to our strategic goals and national values. In closing, I recommend that the Bush administration clearly go on record in opposition to the use of interrogational torture. Additionally, I recommend the Bush administration establish a clear definition of what does and does not constitute torture and the agencies responsible for national security should establish guidelines for interrogation in accordance with that definition.

TABLE OF CONTENTS

PREFACE

Why write about torture? That is a question I have asked myself numerous times during the process of researching and writing this paper. No human act is more universally condemned and yet we can't seem to eradicate its use. While torture is a difficult subject to deal with, incidents such as the abuses at Abu Ghraib caused me to delve further into the subject. Initially, I had no intention of making torture the subject of my student research project but merely wanted to attempt to come to grips with the issue at a personal level. While delving into the subject, I became aware of the "ticking bomb" scenario as a potential justification for the use of torture against terrorists. While this seemed a plausible academic exercise, it didn't really hit home for me until I happened across an episode of *Fox* television's *Twenty-Four*.

In this particular episode, Jack Bauer, a special agent with the fictional Los Angeles Counterterrorism Unit, is faced with the ultimate "ticking bomb" scenario. Bauer captures Said Ali, the leader of the Second Wave terrorist cell and mastermind of a plot to explode a nuclear weapon in Los Angeles. As Bauer begins his interrogation, it becomes apparent that Said Ali is not going to willingly disclose any information. Although unspoken, Bauer has made the decision to use any means necessary to extract the information necessary to prevent a catastrophe and has obviously beaten Ali, yet Ali refuses to divulge the location of the weapon. As the interrogation continues, Bauer has police officers setup television equipment in the room and lets Ali know that security forces in his home country have his family in their custody and that they are awaiting word from Bauer to begin killing members of the family. Ali still refuses to talk. The television comes on and we see Ali's wife and three children tied to chairs and being "roughly" handled by armed masked-men. At the this point in the show, Bauer receives a phone call from the President of the United States who has just learned of Bauer's plans to execute Ali's family members in an effort to get him to reveal the location of the nuclear weapon. The President makes it very clear that he doesn't approve of Bauer's tactics. Bauer makes the decision to proceed anyway and allows Ali to believe the President has approved the action. After making one final plea for Ali to reveal the location of the weapon, Bauer orders the men on the television to shoot Ali's youngest son. When Bauer threatens to have his other son killed, Ali reveals the location of the weapon and the plan for it to be exploded in a small plane over Los Angeles. We later discover that the shootings were staged and that Ali's son was still alive.

After viewing this episode, all I could think is, "Wow, this isn't too far-fetched a concept." With that revelation and in light of Abu Ghraib and our ongoing War on Terror, writing about torture made perfect sense to me. Yes, torture is a dark, difficult subject, but not talking about it or ignoring the fact that it occurs does not make it go away. As I state in my paper, I am not an ethicist, philosopher, or even a lawyer and I have no real expertise in the subject. It is my sincerest hope that my wrestling with this issue may cause others to pause and also give the subject some thought.

TORTURE AND THE WAR ON TERRORISM: TIME TO THINK THE UNTHINKABLE?

> The reason the United States should not torture prisoners is not because it doesn't work. It is simply because it is wrong. It dehumanizes us, undermines our cause, and, over the long term, breeds more enemies of the United States than coercive measures will ever allow us to capture.
>
> —Chris Mackey and Greg Miller, *The Interrogators*

In late April 2004, CBS News' *60 Minutes II* etched Abu Ghraib prison on the collective memory of the world when they released a series of shocking photos depicting the abuse of Iraqi prisoners by U.S. soldiers. American and world opinion erupted in an outpouring of dismay and disgust at the very un-American behavior. The revelation of abuse at Abu Ghraib could not have come at a more "inopportune" time for the Bush administration. With rising U.S. casualties and waning support for the war in Iraq both at home and abroad, the Abu Ghraib scandal has served to strengthen opposition to U.S. involvement in Iraq and caused many to question U.S motives around the world.

Whether the acts committed at Abu Ghraib constitute torture or humiliation; whether institutionally sanctioned up the chain of command or merely the depraved acts of a small group of sadistic individuals are questions beyond the intent of this paper. That the acts occurred is certainly beyond question and that certainty gives rise to some questions of strategic import that warrant further critical analysis—most importantly, should the U.S. sanction the use of torture tactics in its efforts to defeat the forces of global terrorism? I am not a lawyer, ethicist, or philosopher, but as a serving member of the U.S. military, it is my position that the U.S. must maintain an absolute legal ban on the use of coercive interrogation means. I believe this legal ban can be enforced and maintained while still allowing for extraordinary measures to be taken in response to a "ticking bomb" scenario. This paper begins with a brief review of the events leading up to the scandal at Abu Ghraib to include the potential influence of policy discussions at the highest levels of government. Following that background discussion, I identify some of the pitfalls associated with defining torture and review some of the major schools of thought on the subject. In closing I examine the completely antithetical nature of the use of torture in relation to our strategic goals and national values.

THE ROAD TO ABU GHRAIB

The Second Gulf War began on March 19, 2003 and within weeks the U.S. led coalition captured Baghdad and defeated the Iraqi army. Even though all major elements of the Iraqi army were summarily defeated, the coalition soon found itself embroiled in devastating counterinsurgency effort which is ongoing today. Human intelligence is a key component in any fight against an insurgency and the fight against the insurgents in Iraq was no different. As the coalition became more embroiled in the insurgency and the demands for human intelligence increased exponentially, the Abu Ghraib prison scandal hit the headlines.

While the U.S. public and the world first became aware of the abuses committed at Abu Ghraib when *60 Minutes II* first broadcast the stunning photographs from the prison in April 2004, the story of the Abu Ghraib scandal really began in August, 2003. On August 4, 2003, the coalition *reopened* Abu Ghraib[1], a decision that was questioned by many at the time. Under Saddam's rule, Abu Ghraib had been the site of untold tortures, maimings and killings—U.S. soldiers discovered nearly 1000 unmarked graves surrounding the facility soon after the invasion of Iraq (these appear to be a mere fraction of the Iraqis killed there by Sadaam's regime).[2] Soon after the facility was reopened the population of the prison exploded upwards of more than 4,000 prisoners and even though the facility had been refurbished to "bring it up to Western standards," it became apparent within weeks of the reopening that some of the "activities" occurring at the prison fell quite short of Western standards.[3]

On January 13, 2004, at least one soldier from the 372nd Military Police Company had seen enough and filed a report claiming prisoner abuse.[4] His report included a compact disk with hundreds of shocking photographs documenting the abuse of Iraqi prisoners by U.S. soldiers and civilian contractors, many of which would end up on the *60 Minutes II* report in April 2004. The photographs generated a series of investigations into the conduct of U.S. personnel at the prison which resulted in the Taguba report, the Fay-Jones report, the Schlesinger report, the Department of the Army Inspector General report, and at least 7 other investigations which are ongoing today. Even though the findings of the different investigative bodies vary somewhat, all of them seem to at least imply a lack of clear guidance from the highest levels of leadership, so it is instructive at this point to review the guidance propagated by U.S. strategic leadership.

THE MEMO TRAIL

Prior to the terrorist attacks on September 11, 2001, there appeared to be little doubt as to official U.S. policy on the use of torture or abusive techniques during interrogations—captives of the U.S. government were to be treated humanely and in accordance with international laws and conventions. This policy was and is further delineated in military doctrine. U.S. Army Field Manual 34-52 (*FM 34-52*), *Intelligence Interrogation*—the Army's interrogation bible, clearly

2

states in the opening chapter, "…US policy expressly prohibits acts of violence or intimidation, including physical or mental torture, threats, insults, or exposure to inhumane treatment as a means of or aid to interrogation."[5] (*FM 34-52* specifically prohibits pain induced by chemicals or bondage; forcing an individual to stand, sit, or kneel in abnormal positions for prolonged periods of time, food deprivation, any form of beating, mock executions, sleep deprivation, and chemically induced psychosis).[6] Following the 9/11 attack though, the White House and key members of the Bush administration began exploring "options" to its interrogation policy.

On January 18, 2002, at the request of President Bush, the U.S. Justice Department issued a legal opinion discussing the status of Al Qaeda and Taliban prisoners under the Geneva Conventions.[7] This memorandum began a series of discussions between key figures in the Bush administration and the Justice Department which in effect authorized abuse of Al Qaeda and Taliban captives. This series of discussions culminated in a March 6, 2003 draft memorandum entitled, "Working Group Report on Detainee Interrogations in the Global War on Terrorism."[8] *Newsweek* reporter Michael Hirsh claims that this 56-page draft memo, along with other memos from the Justice Department, formed the legal arguments justifying intense interrogation methods (many of those outlined in the paragraph above) used at Guantánamo Bay and that some of those same methods were later used at Abu Ghraib prison.[9] The Bush administration maintains that in spite of the legal discussions contained in these memos, they do not condone torture.[10] Almost a year prior to "Working Group Report…," President Bush made his thoughts on this legal "exercise" clear in a memo dated February 7 2002 when he stated: "Of course, our values as a Nation, values that we share with many nations in the world, call for us to treat detainees humanely, including those who are not legally entitled to such treatment. Our nation has been and will continue to be a strong supporter of Geneva and its principles."[11]

And yet, in spite of President Bush's unambiguous statements in support of humane treatment of detainees, there remained significant ambiguity in U.S. policy on the use of coercive measures. In part, this uncertainty resulted from the approval of techniques beyond those permitted in *FM 34-52* for use against hardcore Al Qaeda/Taliban detainees held at Guantánamo. According to the Independent Panel chaired by former Secretary of State James Schlesinger, "Although specifically limited by the Secretary of Defense to Guantánamo, and requiring his personal approval (given in only two cases), the augmented techniques for Guantánamo migrated to Afghanistan and Iraq where they were neither limited nor safeguarded."[12]

3

DEFINING TORTURE

Webster's *Dictionary* defines torture as, "...the act of inflicting excruciating pain, especially as a means of punishment or coercion; extreme anguish of body or mind."[13] In the *Convention against Torture and Other Cruel, Inhuman or Degrading Treatment or Punishment* "...the term 'torture' means any act by which severe pain or suffering, whether physical or mental, is intentionally inflicted on a person..."[14] In 1994, the U.S. Congress defined torture as: "an act committed by a person acting under the color of law specifically intended to inflict severe physical or mental pain or suffering..."[15] These are but three of the more commonly acknowledged definitions of torture in use today. While all three adequately capture the gravity of the term, they all rely on quantifiers such as *severe* and *excruciating*. Herein lies one of the key "rubs" in current debates on the topic of torture—who or what defines the level of intensity required for pain to reach the threshold of *severe* or *excruciating*?

Senior U.S. leadership has certainly wrestled with defining that threshold in their efforts to broaden the range of tools available to U.S. interrogators. In what is commonly referred to as the *Bybee Memo*, Assistant Attorney General Jay Bybee attempted to narrow the definition of torture to a much more specific range of acts which in effect, would allow U.S. interrogators to apply techniques not previously considered within the guidelines of current laws and regulations. In that memo, which was prepared for the Counsel to the President, Alberto Gonzales, he wrote that "Physical pain amounting to torture must be equivalent in intensity to the pain accompanying serious physical injury, such as organ failure, impairment of bodily function, or even death."[16] While it appears that U.S. interrogators where never given the license to take interrogations to the extremes implied in the *Bybee Memo*, there were definitely instances in which they were authorized to exceed the limits established in *FM 34-52* and it appears that this "mismatch" between military doctrine and U.S. policy was at least in part responsible for the scandal at Abu Ghraib.

This debate over definition is fundamental to any discussion of torture and the potential for its use. I argue below that the clearest path for the U.S. is to adhere to the currently agreed upon standards within U.S. and international law instead of seeking loopholes and workarounds. Before proceeding further with that discussion though let's take a look at three of the leading thinkers on the subject: Marcy Strauss and the absolutist position, Alan Dershowitz and his "torture warrant", and Oren Gross and his thoughts on pragmatic absolutism and official disobedience.

THE ABSOLUTE BAN ON TORTURE

In her 2004 essay entitled "Torture," Marcy Strauss, Professor of Law at Loyola Law School, makes the case for an absolute ban on the use of torture. In light of recent misconduct of U.S. interrogators and military police at Abu Ghraib and Guantánamo, Dr. Strauss explores both the moral and legal implications of the use of interrogational torture and categorically concludes that, "...official state sanctioning of torture is never justified."[17] Her argument is founded on four key findings—the inefficacy of torture, alternative investigative techniques, the negative impact of torture use on society, and the likelihood of increased resort to torture—each of which is discussed in detail below.[18]

Dr. Strauss sites numerous works in support of her assertion that torture, in many cases, just does not work. The common thread in those works is that eventually almost all subjects will "talk" in response to torture. Whether or not they say anything of real value is the fundamental issue. More often than not the individual will say anything in order to stop the torture. In many cases the individual will not have the information the interrogators are seeking but the interrogator will continue to torture in the belief that the individual is "holding out." It is likely that the individual will eventually tell the interrogator what he wants to hear in order to gain some relief from the torture. Strauss asserts that no one can say with 100% that torture never works, but that torture in most cases is ineffective.[19]

Strauss' second point, that torture should not be sanctioned because alternative investigative techniques are usually more efficacious, receives much more detailed treatment in her draft work "The Lessons of Abu Ghraib," in which she states, "...most professional interrogators know that instead of torturing, sophisticated psychological strategies and inducements are often more effective."[20] In *The Interrogators*, Chris Miller, a U.S. Army interrogator who served in Afghanistan in the early days of Operation Enduring Freedom, provides numerous examples of U.S. successes using methods other than physical torture. "One of our biggest successes in Afghanistan," he write, "came when a valuable prisoner decided to cooperate not because he had been abused (he had not been), but precisely because he realized he would not be tortured.[21] We dealt with the enemy justly and humanely. We practiced methods of interrogation that were long on trickery and deceit, but we never touched anyone."[22]

To support her third finding that the use of torture negatively impacts society, Dr. Strauss quotes Mordecai Kremnitzer, an Israeli lawyer writing on the Landau Commission's findings (the Landau Commission was convened in 1987 to investigate reports of Israeli use of torture in interrogations): "When the state itself beats and extorts, it can no longer be said to rest on foundations of morality and justice, but rather on force. When a state [employs] torture, it reduces the moral distance between government act and criminal act."[23] In effect, the state loses the moral high-ground if it allows its agents resort to the tactics of torture. As Strauss puts it, "...we would be 'lowering' ourselves to the same level as the terrorists if we were to engage in state-sanctioned terror."[24]

Strauss' fourth and final finding centers on the "slippery slope" argument. While acknowledging that "...virtually no one seriously advocates the wholesale use of torture," she is concerned with the "ticking bomb" scenario, i.e. If we allow for a narrowly defined situation in which torture is permissible, is there a means by which we could prevent the spread of the use of torture to lesser situations? The ticking bomb scenario posits a case in which a known terrorist or his associate is captured and is in possession of the knowledge required to prevent a catastrophic event from occurring, i.e., the explosion of a suitcase nuclear device in Manhattan. Some would argue that in this case interrogators would be justified in using extraordinary means to obtain that information from the suspect, i.e., torture. Strauss argues that, "...no matter how one tries to confine the use of torture to extreme, narrow circumstances, the temptation to broaden those circumstances is inevitable."[25] She goes on to say, "Without an absolute prohibition on the use of torture, it is virtually impossible to ensure that 'special cases' remain special."[26]

Dr. Strauss presents a compelling argument in support of her thesis that there should be an absolute ban on interrogational torture, until one delves further into her rendering of the catastrophic terrorist situation. It is at this point that the most significant shortfall in her absolutist position reveals itself. She argues that even though interrogative torture may prevent the catastrophic loss of life in the ticking bomb scenario, that we should not entertain creating an exception to a no torture policy because, "...it is my strong belief that this hypothetical (ticking bomb), would almost certainly, never happen."[27] Even though her assertion may be true, it seems at the very least, intellectually perilous to avoid addressing the use of interrogational torture in the catastrophic situation by denying the possibility of its potential occurrence. Strauss also applies this same line of reasoning to Alan Dershowitz' "torture warrant" theory and although she denies the utility of this theory based on the unlikely occurrence of a ticking bomb event, it is of value to take a closer look at his theory.

DERSHOWITZ AND THE "TORTURE WARRANT"

In *Why Terrorism Works: Understanding the Threat, Responding to the Challenge,* Alan Dershowitz, well-known civil libertarian lawyer and professor of law at Harvard Law School, poses the question, "Should the ticking bomb terrorist be tortured?"[28] Dershowitz posits that in the ticking bomb scenario, public officials would seek a "torture warrant" in order to legally employ interrogational torture much in the same manner that search warrants are issued today. While this proposition has generated significant controversy amongst lawyers and philosophers alike, it certainly warrants further examination.

Dershowitz first used the term "torture warrant" in the 1980s while conducting research and teaching at Hebrew University in Israel.[29] It was during this period that he became aware that the Israeli GSS was using the techniques described previously in an attempt to obtain information from terrorist suspects in order to prevent future attacks. As Dershowitz discussed the use of "moderate physical pressure" with his students, he soon discovered that while some took issue with the routine use of these methods, almost no one took issue with the use of such techniques in order to prevent a potentially catastrophic ticking bomb event.[30] He also came to the realization that the "...hypothetical ticking bomb terrorist was serving as a moral, intellectual, and legal justification for a pervasive system of coercive interrogation, which, though not the paradigm of torture, certainly bordered on it."[31] It was in the light of this discovery that he asked his students, "If the reason you permit nonlethal torture is based on the ticking bomb case, why not limit it exclusively to that compelling but rare situation?"[32] He further challenged that "...if you believe that nonlethal torture is justifiable in the ticking bomb case, why not require advance judicial approval—a 'torture warrant'?"[33] Public criticism of Dershowitz' theory, especially from the media, was immediate and persistent.

In an attempt to clarify his position, Dershowitz went on to develop the idea of a torture warrant in numerous writings, probably most succinctly in a 2004 article for the New York Law School Law Review in response to Marcy Strauss' essay entitled "Torture," from the same journal. In, "The Torture Warrant: A Response to Professor Strauss," he writes:

> I am generally against torture as a normative matter, and I would like to see its use minimized. I believe that at least moderate forms of non-lethal torture are in fact being used by the United States and some of its allies today. I think that if we ever confronted an actual case of imminent mass terrorism that could be prevented by the infliction of torture we would use torture, (even lethal torture), and the public would favor its use.[34]

He continues in the next paragraph:

> I pose the issue as follows: If torture is in fact being used and/or would in fact be used in an actual ticking bomb mass terrorism case, would it be normatively better or worse to have such torture regulated by some kind of warrant, with accountability, record-keeping, standards, and limitations...It is not so much about the substantive issue of torture, as it is over accountability, visibility, and candor in a democracy that is confronting a choice of evils.[35]

7

Although Dershowitz feels that the torture warrant is probably the best alternative to deal with the ticking bomb case, he readily admits that greatest fault in his theory is that it legitimizes abhorrent practice, but in his words, "...better to legitimate and control a *specific* practice that will occur, than to legitimate a *general* practice of tolerating extra-legal actions under the table of scrutiny and beneath the radar screen of accountability."[36]

Dershowitz is not alone in his conviction that there are situations in which we may have to do the unthinkable. In "Torture: Thinking the Unthinkable," Andrew McCarthy takes Dershowitz' theory to the next level. McCarthy agrees with Dershowitz' proposition that there are situations in which we would be better served allowing the use of interrogational torture under the strict monitoring of the judicial system rather than turning an institutional blind-eye, but he also believes that we have to rethink our entire judicial system in light of the current war on terrorism. He proposes the establishment of a "national security court."[37] Under his concept, "This would be a tribunal, drawn from the national pool of federal judges, that would have jurisdiction over, and develop an expertise in, matters of national security."[38] This national security tribunal would be charged with monitoring the detention of terrorists and conducting the trials of those "...whom the government elected to charge under special rules that would apply only in national security cases."[39] This tribunal would also be the body responsible to consider the issuance of torture warrants and to monitor their execution. In McCarthy's view, establishing this national level tribunal would provide even greater oversight and transparency to the use of torture warrants and would also develop a body of judges with experience in their application.

Even with this greater level of oversight though, there are issues which remain unresolved. Oren Gross, a law professor at University of Minnesota Law School, presents numerous "problematic" issues with the torture warrant proposition in his article, "Are Torture Warrants Warranted?", key of which is the legitimization of torture. Gross' contention is that the potential use of interrogational torture is a virtual moral, social, political, and legal minefield. While he agrees with Dershowitz that extreme situations may occur in which the use of interrogational torture is warranted, Gross argues that it should be accomplished under the guise of *official disobedience*.

PRAGMATIC ABSOLUTISM AND OFFICIAL DISOBEDIENCE

Gross makes the argument that one can have an absolute legal prohibition on torture without arbitrarily dismissing the "ticking bomb" scenario. In "The Prohibition on Torture and the Limits of the Law", he argues that supporting an absolute ban on torture versus a conditional ban (Alan Dershowitz' "torture warrant"), is the only appropriate course legally and morally. He does acknowledge though that a truly catastrophic situation, e.g. the "ticking bomb" scenario, may lead public officials to act outside the law and in some instances, even to violate the absolute prohibition on torture by employing *preventive interrogational torture*. Gross defines preventive interrogational torture as torture used to gain information that would aid in the prevention of catastrophic terrorist attacks.[40]

Gross' thesis, which he refers to as *pragmatic absolutism* and *official disobedience*, posits that we can have an absolute legal ban on the use of interrogational torture while allowing that in some instances the resort to torture may be defensible (pragmatic absolutism) and that government officials may find it necessary to violate that legal ban (official disobedience) in those instances. His position is that are many arguments in support of the absolute legal ban on torture, the four most significant of which are summarized below:

- *Setting general policy; accommodating exceptional cases*—While catastrophic situations may require extralegal actions, those situations are extremely rare. Instead of enacting law based on those rare instances, Gross argues that we "...must be mindful of the risk of creating bad law (and ethics) to answer the particular needs of the hard case."[41]

- *Symbolism, myths, and education*—Gross contends that an absolute legal ban on the use of torture is, "...desirable in order to uphold the symbolism of human dignity and the inviolability of the human body."[42] He goes on to state that, "...even if one believes that the absolute legal prohibition on torture is unrealistic, as a practical matter, there is independent value in upholding the myth that torture is absolutely prohibited," and that, "...such a position provides obvious notice that fundamental rights and values are not forsaken, whatever the circumstances, and that cries of national security, emergency, and catastrophe do not trump fundamental liberties."[43] He goes on to say, "The more entrenched a norm is—and the prohibition on torture is among the most entrenched ones—the harder it will be for the government to convince the public that violating the norm is necessary."[44] Maintaining an absolute ban on torture also sends a clear signal to other nations that such practices are impermissible.

- *Strategy of resistance*—Gross argues that even though the use of preventive interrogational torture may be inevitable, maintaining the absolute prohibition on such techniques may be the best strategy for preventing the use of interrogational torture in "...less-than-catastrophic cases or against persons who are not 'suspected terrorists'."[45] He contends that maintaining an absolute legal prohibition may deter government officials from resorting to interrogational torture even in the truly

9

exceptional cases by imposing moral inhibitions and allowing for the possibility of criminal prosecution if the acts are later deemed unnecessary. [46] While on the surface this may appear to be a variation of the "slippery slope" argument, the real point of the discussion is that even if we conclude that the use of torture is inevitable (i.e. the ticking bomb scenario), we should continue the absolute legal prohibition in order to resist the prevalence of the use of torture.

- *Rejection of balancing tests*—"Balancing" occurs when the prohibition on torture is weighed against competing values, for example, when the use of torture to prevent the loss of life is weighed against the individual right to not be tortured. When the "balance" is in the favor of preventing catastrophe, the interrogator is "justified" in torturing. This type of balancing is subject to biases, factually difficult to accomplish and will usually lead to more torture rather than less. Maintaining the absolute legal prohibition on torture does not allow for balancing, at least in a legal sense. Gross' official disobedience certainly requires moral balancing on the part of government officials though.

According to Gross, it is at this point that, "Most absolutists end the discussion of the permissibility of interrogational torture."[47] For him though, the discussion merely begins at this point and his insistence on continuing the discussion is what puts the "pragmatism" in his pragmatic absolutist thesis. In Gross' words, "To deny the use of preventive interrogational torture, even when, for example, there is good reason to believe that a massive bomb is ticking in a mall is as coldhearted as it is to permit torture in the first place. It is cold hearted because in the true catastrophic cases the failure to use preventive interrogational torture will result in the death of many innocent people."[48] In an attempt to reconcile the dilemma created by the absolute ban on torture and the need to respond to catastrophic attacks, Gross offers the concept of official disobedience.

Gross' theory of official disobedience recognizes the absolute ban on torture and yet also recognizes that the use of preventive interrogational torture in extreme cases such as the ticking bomb scenario may be deemed a necessity by government officials. Official disobedience does not provide legal authorization *a priori*, that is, in advance of the occurrence of a catastrophic event, but does acknowledge that some situations may be so extreme as to lead a public official to act outside of the law. If the situation requires the use interrogational torture to prevent a catastrophic event, the official may do so with the understanding that they will be held responsible for their extralegal actions after the fact—in effect, the public official is required to balance the absolute ban on torture against the perceived need to take extralegal action in order to prevent the catastrophic event. Official disobedience does not provide legal accommodation for the use of torture as does Dershowitz' torture warrant, but requires public officials seek *ex post* ratification for their actions from both a judge and jury or via some form of executive pardon. This ratification or pardon does not remove the illegality of the public official's actions, it merely acknowledges the necessity of those actions in the event under scrutiny.

The requirement for *ex post* ratification versus *a priori* approval, as spelled out by Gross, provides "checks-and-balances" on the use of preventive interrogational torture. Public officials will be rightly hesitant to use preventive interrogational torture, even in extreme cases, because "...the official who decides to use torture undertakes a significant risk because of the uncertain prospects for subsequent public ratification."[49] Even if public ratification is obtained and the official is protected from criminal charges, he may not be shielded from torture victims seeking settlement in civil court. Domestic ratification does not relieve the official (and the nation) from potential international sanctions. Because ratification for the actions must come *ex post* there is little chance of the establishment of legal precedent for the use of interrogational torture. It is obvious from these points and many others Gross presents that the decision to participate in extralegal interrogation practices is not one that will be made lightly.

Gross acknowledges that his theory of absolute pragmatism and official disobedience may appear to be a case of "...trying to have his cake and eating it too."[50] While there may be an element of truth in that assessment, Gross presents a compelling argument that attempts to realistically deal with one of the more fundamentally troubling issues of our time. As Gross himself points out, "The prohibition on torture and the catastrophic case present us with truly tragic choices...we may as well make such decisions in as informed a manner as possible...it is in this context that public debate on torture is critical."[51] It is with this thought in mind that we now turn to recommendations for U.S. strategic leadership as we continue our war on global terrorism.

WHY MAINTAIN AN ABSOLUTE BAN ON TORTURE

The terrorist attacks on September 11, 2001 made it painfully clear that the U.S., and indeed the world, faces a troubling and potentially devastating menace in the guise of global terrorism. This fight against global terrorism requires us to rethink our methods and tactics in order to better protect individual freedoms and the right to live free from terror. In spite of the new character of this threat though, we must not allow ourselves to resort to tactics of terror such as torture. In response to this new threat President George W. Bush released *The National Security Strategy of the United States of America* (September 2002). This document

11

lays the foundation for our global war on terrorism and in broad terms, describes the U.S. vision of how that effort will be accomplished. While the document presents some previously unstated concepts such as preemption[52], it remains fundamentally committed to human rights and the respect for human dignity above all else—"Our goals on the path to progress are clear…to achieve these goals, the United States will champion aspirations for human dignity."[53] In Chapter 2, President Bush goes on to state, "In the war against global terrorism, we will never forget that we are ultimately fighting for our *democratic values and way of life* (emphasis added)."[54]

The current war on terrorism has been depicted as many different things but fundamentally it is a war of ideas—primarily democracy vs. fear—and while we may not be losing the war outright, we are definitely not winning it either. Most certainly the legal interpretations (Gonzales memo, Bybee memo, and others), rendered at the highest levels of U.S. government, of the legal limits on interrogation and the status of detainees strengthens the impression that we are self-serving and do not live up to the values espoused not only in *The National Security Strategy of the United States of America*, but fundamental founding documents such as the Declaration of Independence and the U.S. Constitution. This impression is prevalent around the globe and is probably the single greatest challenge we face in this war of ideas.

Even before the revelation of the abuses at Abu Ghraib it was apparent that America's image around the globe was taking a beating. In "Can America Regain Its Soft Power After Abu Ghraib," Joseph Nye presents some very sobering figures—"…anti-Americanism had been rising around the world. Polls showed that the United States lost some thirty points of attraction in Europe in 2003, and America's standing had plummeted in the Islamic world from Morocco to Indonesia."[55]

While the apparent loss of prestige in Europe is disappointing, Hisham Melhem, the Washington correspondent for the Beirut newspaper *Al-Safir*, paints an even grimmer picture when asked during an interview how the Arab street reacted to the abuses at Abu Ghraib:

> If you wanted to write a script or a scenario as to how you undermine the credibility of the United States in the Middle East today, you couldn't have done a better job…I think one could argue *if you have any illusions about winning the hearts and minds in Iraq and the Arab world for that matter, you should forget that* (emphasis added).[56]

Later in the interview, Melham goes on to add, "Sometimes I wonder the people in Washington have *no clue as to what their policies are doing in the Arab and Muslim world* (emphasis added)."[57]

It is obvious that whether or not the abuses at Abu Ghraib were officially sanctioned is of relatively little significance in this discussion of our war of ideas. What is of significance is that these abuses occurred under U.S. auspices and that, in the minds of many, they equate to the U.S. sanctioning the use of torture.

CONCLUSION

In his classic essay on the subject, "Torture," Henry Shue poses the question, "...if practically everyone is opposed to all torture, why bring it up, start people thinking about it, and risk weakening the inhibitions against what is clearly a terrible business?"[58] As I stated earlier, I am not a lawyer, ethicist, or philosopher, but it is clear to me that we must address the subject of torture in an honest, open fashion. As Oren Gross put it, "By not discussing the practice of torture we do not make it go away; we drive it underground."[59] Recent events such as the shameful occurrences at Abu Ghraib make it painfully obvious that we have not made torture go away.

We are faced with a different sort of threat in the Global War on Terror which has caused those responsible for national security and the well-being of U.S. citizens to rethink the tactics and methods employed to defeat global terrorists. Obviously discussions on the subject of interrogational torture have occurred at the highest levels of U.S. government and in the halls of academia. What remains to be accomplished is to turn those ruminations in to a clearly stated national position on the subject. Although Strauss' position of absolute prohibition appears to be most in-line with our national values, her theory does not adequately address the catastrophic ticking bomb scenario, which one could argue we are likely to face in the future. While permitting the use of interrogational torture in the ticking bomb scenario may indeed lead to the temptation to expand its use to lesser scenarios as she asserts, one could argue that our legal system is certainly capable of limiting that temptation as does Alan Dershowitz. Dershowitz' torture warrant more adequately addresses the ticking bomb issue yet verges on legitimizing and institutionalizing the practice of torture. While Gross' theory of absolute prohibition and official disobedience may appear to be the proverbial attempt at having the cake and eating too, it also appears to offer the best guidelines for our national leadership and should be used as a basis for further discussions of the subject.

President Bush and other senior members of government have publicly stated that the U.S. is firmly opposed to the use of torture in numerous speeches, yet many of the memorandums written by members of this same group have created grave doubts as to our true position. The current situation presents an ideal opportunity for the administration to go on

13

record in opposition to the use of interrogational torture. Additionally, the Bush administration should establish a clear definition of what does and does not constitute torture and the agencies responsible for national security should establish guidelines for interrogation in accordance with that definition.

WORD COUNT=5983

ENDNOTES

[1] *Washington Post*, "Chronology of Abu Ghraib," 9 May 2004; available from http://www.washingtonpost.com/wp-srv/world/daily/graphics/abughraib_050904.htm; Internet; accessed 1 October 2004.

[2] Roger Cohen, "Iraq's Abu Ghraib Prison Should Be Closed Now," *International Herald Tribune*, 4 May 2004; available from <http://www.iht.com/articles/518229.html>; Internet; accessed 8 September 2004.

[3] Ibid.

[4] *Washington Post*.

[5] Department of the Army, *Intelligence Interrogation*, Army Field Manual 34-52 (Washington, D.C.: U.S. Department of the Army, 28 September 1992), 1-8.

[6] Ibid., 1-8.

[7] Michael Ratner, "Bush Administration Memos on Torture Policy Reveal Official Complicity in Abuse of Iraqi Prisoners," interview by Scott Harris, *Scoop,* 23 June 2004; available from <http://www.scoop.co.nz/mason/stories/HL0406/S00202.htm>; Internet; accessed 27 September 2004.

[8] Michael Hirsh, "New Torture Furor: A Defense Department Memo Provides Legal Roadmap For Prisoner Interrogation," *Newsweek*, 8 June 2004; available from <http://www.msnbc.msn.com/id/5167122/site/newsweek/>; Internet; accessed 27 September 2004.

[9] Ibid.

[10] Ibid.

[11] President George W. Bush, "Humane Treatment of al Qaeda and Taliban Detainees," memorandum for the Vice President, Washington, D.C., 7 February 2002; available from <http://www.swem.wm.edu/GOVDOC/govinfo.htm>; Internet; accessed 1 Oct 2004.

[12] Steven Strasser, ed., *The Abu Ghraib Investigations* (New York: PublicAffairs, 2004), xx.

[13] *Random House Webster's Dictionary*, (New York: Ballantine Books, 2001), 755.

[14] United Nations, "Convention against Torture and Other Cruel, Inhuman or Degrading Treatment or Punishment," 1984; available from <http://www1.umn.edu/humanrts/instree/h2catoc.htm>; Internet; accessed 26 November 2004.

[15] *Crimes And Criminal Procedure, U.S. Code*, Title 18, secs. 2340-2340A (1994).

[16] Mark Danner, *Torture and Truth: America, Abu Ghraib, and the War on Terror*, (New York: New York Review of Books, 2004), 115.

[17] Marcy S. Strauss, "Torture," *New York Law School Law Review*, vol. 48, nos. 1&2 (2003/2004), 208; available from <http://www.nyls.edu/pdfs/v48n1-2p201-274.pdf>; Internet; accessed 10 October 2004.

[18] Ibid., 208.

[19] Marcy S. Strauss, "The Lessons of Abu Ghraib," *Ohio State Law Journal*, vol. 66 (2005), 39; available from <http://papers.ssrn.com/sol3/papers.cfm?abstract_id=597061>; Internet; accessed 20 October 2004.

[20] Ibid., 37.

[21] Chris Mackey and Greg Miller, *The Interrogators* (New York: Little, Brown and Company, 2004), xxiii.

[22] Ibid., 468.

[23] Strauss, "The Lessons of Abu Ghraib," 254.

[24] Ibid., 256.

[25] Ibid., 267.

[26] Ibid.

[27] Ibid., 270.

[28] Alan M. Dershowitz, *Why Terrorism Works* (London, CT: R.R. Donnelly & Sons Co., 2002), 131.

[29] Ibid., 139.

[30] Ibid., 140.

[31] Ibid.

[32] Ibid., 141.

[33] Ibid.

[34] Alan Dershowitz, "The Torture Warrant: A Response to Professor Strauss," *New York Law School Law Review*, vol. 48, nos. 1&2 (2003/2004), 277; available from < http://www.nyls.edu/pdfs/v48n1-2p275-294.pdf>; Internet; accessed 24 October 2004.

[35] Ibid., 277-278.

[36] Ibid., 283.

[37] Andrew C. McCarthy, "Torture: Thinking About The Unthinkable," *Commentary*, July-August 2004; available from <http://www.benadorassociates.com/article/5900>; Internet; accessed 19 October 2004.

[38] Ibid.

[39] Ibid.

[40] Oren Gross, "The Prohibition on Torture and the Limits of the Law," in *Torture: A Collection*, ed. Sanford Levinson (New York: Oxford University Press, 2004), 232.

[41] Ibid., 234.

[42] Ibid.

[43] Ibid., 234-235.

[44] Ibid., 235.

[45] Ibid.

[46] Ibid.

[47] Ibid., 236.

[48] Ibid., 237.

[49] Ibid., 244.

[50] Ibid., 248.

[51] Ibid., 249

[52] George W. Bush, *The National Security Strategy of the United States of America* (Washington D.C.: The White House, September 2002), 15.

[53] Ibid., 1.

[54] Ibid., 7.

[55] Joseph S. Nye, Jr., "Can America Regain Its Soft Power After Abu Ghraib?" *Yale Global*, 29 July 2004; available from http://yaleglobal.yale.edu/display.article?id=4302; Internet; accessed 8 September 2004.

[56] Ray Suarez, "Prisoner Abuse Fallout," *NewsHour With Jim Lehrer* (interview transcript), 3 May 2004; available from http://www.pbs.org/newshour/bb/middle_east/jan-june04/photos_5-3.html; Internet; accessed 8 September 2004.

[57] Ibid.

[58] Henry Shue, "Torture," in *Torture: A Collection*, ed. Sanford Levinson (New York: Oxford University Press, 2004), 47.

[59] Gross, "The Prohibition on Torture and the Limits of the Law," 249.

BIBLIOGRAPHY

Bush, George W. *The National Security Strategy of the United States of America*. Washington D.C.: The White House, September 2002.

_____. "Humane Treatment of al Qaeda and Taliban Detainees." Memorandum for the Vice President. Washington, D.C., 7 February 2002. Available from <http://www.swem.wm.edu/GOVDOC/govinfo.htm>. Internet. Accessed 1 Oct 2004.

Cohen, Roger. "Iraq's Abu Ghraib Prison Should Now Be Closed." *International Herald Tribune*. 4 May 2004. Available from <http://www.iht.com/bin/print.php?file=518229.html>. Internet. Accessed 8 September 2004.

Crimes and Criminal Procedure. *U.S. Code*. Title 18, secs. 2340-2340A (1994).

Danner, Mark. *Torture and Truth: America, Abu Ghraib, and the War on Terror*. New York: New York Review of Books, 2004.

Dershowitz, Alan M. *Why Terrorism Works*. London, CT: R.R. Donnelly & Sons Co., 2002.

_____. "The Torture Warrant: A Response to Professor Strauss." *New York Law School Law Review*, vol. 48, nos. 1&2 (2003/2004): 275-294. Available from <http://www.nyls.edu/pdfs/v48n1-2p275-294.pdf>. Internet. Accessed 24 October 2004.

Gross, Oren. "The Prohibition on Torture and the Limits of the Law." In *Torture: A Collection*, ed. Sanford Levinson, 229-253. New York: Oxford University Press, 2004.

Hirsh, Michael. "New Torture Furor: A Defense Department Memo Provides Legal Roadmap For Prisoner Interrogation." *Newsweek*. 8 June 2004. Available from <http://www.msnbc.msn.com/id/5167122/site/newsweek/>. Internet. Accessed 27 September 2004.

Mackey, Chris and Greg Miller. *The Interrogators*. New York: Little, Brown and Company, 2004.

McCarthy, Andrew C. "Torture: Thinking About The Unthinkable." *Commentary*, July-August 2004. Available from <http://www.benadorassociates.com/article/5900>. Internet. Accessed 19 October 2004.

Nye, Joseph S., Jr. "Can America Regain Its Soft Power After Abu Ghraib?" *Yale Global*, 29 July 2004. Available from <http://yaleglobal.yale.edu/display.article?id=4302>. Internet. Accessed 8 September 2004.

Random House Webster's Dictionary. New York: Ballantine Books, 2001.

Ratner, Michael. "Bush Administration Memos on Torture Policy Reveal Official Complicity in Abuse of Iraqi Prisoners." Interview by Scott Harris. *Scoop*. 23 June 2004. Available from <http://www.scoop.co.nz/mason/stories/HL0406/S00202.htm>. Internet. Accessed 27 September 2004.

Shue, Henry. "Torture." In *Torture: A Collection*, ed. Sanford Levinson, 47-60. New York: Oxford University Press, 2004.

Strasser, Steven, ed. *The Abu Ghraib Investigations*. New York: PublicAffairs, 2004.

Strauss, Marcy. "Torture." *New York Law School Law Review,* vol.48, nos. 1&2 (2003-2004): 201-274. Available from <http://www.nyls.edu/pdfs/v48n1-2p201-274.pdf>. Internet. Accessed 10 October 2004.

_____. "The Lessons of Abu Ghraib." *Ohio State Law Journal*, vol. 66 (2005): 1-50. Available from <http://papers.ssrn.com/sol3/papers.cfm?abstract_id=597061>. Internet. Accessed 20 October 2004.

Suarez, Ray, "Prisoner Abuse Fallout." *NewsHour With Jim Lehrer* (interview transcript), 3 May 2004. Available from <http://www.pbs.org/newshour/bb/middle_east/jan-june04/photos_5-3.html>. Internet. Accessed 8 September 2004.

United Nations. "Convention against Torture and Other Cruel, Inhuman or Degrading Treatment or Punishment," 1984; Available from <http://www1.umn.edu/humanrts/instree/h2catoc.htm>. Internet. Accessed 26 November 2004.

U.S. Department of the Army. *Intelligence Interrogation*. Army Field Manual 34-52. Washington D.C.: U.S. Department of the Army, 28 September 1992.

Washington Post. "Chronology of Abu Ghraib," 9 May 2004. Available from <http://www.washingtonpost.com/wp-srv/world/daily/graphics/abughraib_050904.htm>. Internet. Accessed 1 October 2004.